FOOTPRINTS IN TIME

*A walk where
New Hampshire began*

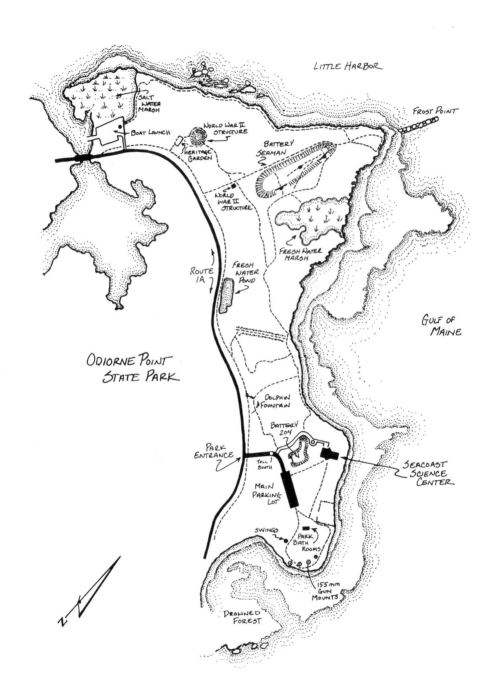

FOOTPRINTS IN TIME

*A walk where
New Hampshire began*

Compiled by Howard S. Crosby, Wendy W. Lull and Richard T. MacIntyre

First published 1994
© Copyright Howard S. Crosby, Wendy W. Lull and Richard T. MacIntyre, 1994

Alan Sutton Limited
12 Riverside Court
Bath BA2 3DZ

ISBN 0 7524 0056 8

Typesetting & origination
by Alan Sutton Limited
Printed in Great Britain

The Seacoast Science Center is open year round. Visitor hours vary seasonally; call 603 436-8043 for current program schedules and hours. Odiorne Point State Park is also ope throughout the year, hours vary seasonally. Park rest room facilities are open spring, summer and fall. For Park information call 603-436-7406, or 603-436-1552.

Contents

Introduction	7
Safety and Conservation Guidelines	9
Seacoast Science Center to the Atlantic Shore Line	11
Atlantic Shore Line to the Gun Mounts	16
Gun Mounts to Battery 204	28
Battery 204 to the Dolphin Fountain	34
Dolphin Fountain to the Odiorne Homestead	38
The Odiorne Homestead to the Pond	44
Pond to the Salt Marsh	54
Salt Marsh to Heritage Garden	56
Heritage Garden to the Plotting Room	60
Plotting Room to Battery Seaman	65
Battery Seaman to Frost Point	70
Frost Point to Battery Seaman	79
Battery Seaman to the McKim/Gage Property	83
The McKim/Gage Property to Columbus Road	95
Bibliography	103

Introduction

This book is the first illustrated walking guide of Odiorne Point State Park, a natural and cultural treasure of New England's seacoast. At last you can discover the fascinating stories of the land and the people who lived here whether you use the book as a guide to park trails, or read it at home.

Seacoast Science Center

The walking tour can be a one-to-two hour stroll, or a lifetime of exploration. (Combined, the history committee has spent over twenty-five years researching Odiorne's past and is constantly discovering new information!) Like the earliest Odiorne inhabitants, no matter which path you choose, you will find many reasons to return. Whether walking or relaxing at home, you are about to meet the courageous settlers who left all they knew for the promise of freedom in this place. You will hear the echoes of later families' aspirations and anger, successes and surrenders as they gave up their homes for their nation's defense.

Odiorne Point State Park has a landscape reflecting thousands of years of change. Your walk begins at the Seacoast Science Center and takes you past ice-age tree stumps, the ruins of once fine estates, and the remains of mighty military fortifications. You will walk

Welcome to the home of the Seacoast Science Center and a treasure of natural, social and military history.

Completed in 1992, the Seacoast Science Center is the third structure at Odiorne Point used for environmental education since World War II.

along breathtaking sea-side vistas, through woodlands and meadows, past ponds and marshes. Afterwards, plan to spend some time with the Seacoast Science Center's exhibits to add to your understanding and enjoyment of the natural and cultural history of Odiorne Point.

This walk has been a popular guided tour since 1988, and is still conducted for park visitors and groups through the Seacoast Science Center. For information, call the Center at 603-436-8043. Enjoy your walk!

The Seacoast Science Center is managed by the Audubon Society of New Hampshire under contract with the State of New Hampshire, in affiliation with the Friends of Odiorne Point, Inc., and the University of New Hampshire Cooperative Extension/Sea Grant Program.

Safety and Conservation Guidelines: Tips to help improve your visit.

Help us retain the natural flavor of Odiorne Point State Park by following these important safety and conservation guidelines.

Around the Park:

1. Take only photographs, leave only footprints. Shells, sticks, flowers and plants are both habitat and food for the creatures that call Odiorne Point home. Hermit crabs live in empty snail shells; birds eat the grubs that burrow in dead sticks. Please honor our ban on collecting materials of all kinds. New Hampshire Parks are carry in/carry-out parks; please take your trash out of the Park and dispose of it properly.

2. When walking on the paved bicycle path, keep an eye and ear out for cyclists and roller-blade skaters.

3. Most of the plants and animals in the Park are not dangerous or poisonous, with the exception of poison ivy, which grows abundantly throughout the Park. There is a description and illustration of poison ivy on page 12 If you think you may have touched some dur-

FOOTPRINTS IN TIME

ing your walk, scrub that part of you carefully with soap and water as soon as you finish your walk. Remember, wild animals tend to bite if provoked or if they feel threatened. For their protection and your own safety, please do not disturb our plants and animals.

4. Odiorne Point is generally a safe park, but it is also a big park. For your own safety, stay on the trails. Remember the gates close at sunset in summer, and earlier in the winter. Gate closing time is posted by the Park entrance.

On the Rocky Shore:

1. Assume slippery rocks! Coastal rocks are often wet from sea spray and can be very slippery. Even when they appear to be dry, take extra care for a sure footing.

2. Always wear sturdy, soft-soled shoes. The rocks may be smooth, but the barnacles are very sharp. Be careful when leaning against a barnacle-covered rock as it is easy to get a nasty scrape.

3. When exploring tide pools, remember to put rocks back bottom-side down where you found them because plants and animals live on rock bottoms and will die if exposed to air and sun too long. If you peek under the long seaweeds, please put these back also.

Seacoast Science Center to the Atlantic Shore Line

Seacoast Science Center to the Atlantic Shore Line

The first part of the Odiorne Point walking tour will take you from the Seacoast Science Center around the southern end of the state park. This section of trail winds past different sites, the stories of which are greatly separated in time. Here too you will have some of New Hampshire's best views of the Atlantic Ocean and the Isles of Shoals.

Your walk starts at the main entrance of the Science Center which encapsulates the summer home Robert Sugden built in 1920. Begin by walking straight ahead

As you exit the Science Center, look to your left for these two posts and proceed down the trail.

FOOTPRINTS IN TIME

and slightly left so that the ocean is on your left. About 30 yards away you will see a set of posts marking a path cut through the omnipresent sumac bush. This is a non-poisonous variety called staghorn because of the pattern and velvety surface of its antler-like branches. Its dull red drupes (fruit) serve as food for many species of birds during the winter and also may be crushed and made into a delightful, tart drink. Sumac bark and leaves have a high concentration of tannic acid that is used for tanning leather.

Staghorn sumac. Much of the area of what is now the Park was covered by the lawns of residential estates prior to World War II. This invasive staghorn sumac rapidly took hold when the lawns were no longer mowed during and following the war.

In addition to the sumac, another abundant plant here is poison ivy. From spring to early fall, walkers in the park with exposed skin should avoid the edges of the paths. Poison ivy may be recognized as a low, three-leaved plant the leaves of which are usually (but not always) shiny.

These paths also can become quite slippery when wet: walk carefully!

The path continues straight ahead for approximately 100 yards. At the end of this path, look left into a grassy area circumscribed by a stone wall.

This site marks the location of a home owned by Kathryn A. Stevens of Belmont, Massachusetts. Built in the 1920s on land purchased from Bertha Sugden, the summer home was one of the eleven homes which stood at Odiorne Point before World War II. A two-story house of seven or eight

Along all of the trails in the Park, you should be on constant lookout for poison ivy with its shiny green leaves in sets of three.

Seacoast Science Center to the Atlantic Shore Line

Now the Park's group picnic area, entry through these stone gate posts was to the Stevens' house.

rooms, the Stevens' home had a glassed-in porch across the ocean side which offered a grand view of the waters at the entrance to Portsmouth Harbor. It was razed by the federal government in 1942.

Odiorne Point is very much a place for the enjoyment of the community, but today this is the only part of the Park which may be reserved for private use. Except during winter months, any day might bring a group gathering, picnic, wedding, or family reunion. This beautiful area is very popular and must be booked well in advance.

Continue walking to the asphalt path and turn left to proceed toward the open ocean. Historically, the area from north of the present Science Center to the cove on the southern rim of the Park was called Odiorne's Point, but local usage has applied the name to the entire peninsula. The asphalt path makes this entire area, including several picnic tables, accessible to those in wheelchairs and the handicapped.

This is the only known photograph of the Stevens' house taken from the vicinity of what is now the Seacoast Science Center.

Seacoast Science Center to the Atlantic Shore Line

The Stevens property was completely surrounded by stone walls. The walls on the seaward side of the house were meant to keep the nor'easters from spraying salt water on the lawn. Over the years, nature has prevailed and the wall has required much repair. Significant repair was required after three "storms of the century" blasted over Odiorne Point in 1992. Note the steps for gaining access to the shore at the right end of the seaward wall.

Handicapped accessible asphalt walk. From the parking lot, people in wheelchairs can make a loop of the south end of the park on the asphalt paths.

Atlantic Shore Line to the Gun Mounts

As you approach the rocky shore the paved path is lined on the left side by a profusion of rose called Rosa rugosa. This variety of rose was introduced from the Orient and thrives in the salt air along the shore line. The fragrance from this flower is an aromatic delight. After the flower petals fall away a small round fruit known as a "rose hip" is visible. The rose hip contains a very high concentration of vitamin C and is often made into a jam or tea enjoyed by health-minded individuals.

The area to your right is the site of another seaside summer home. In 1927, Helen McG. Graves of Contoocook, New Hampshire, purchased the land and together with her husband, Dr. Graves, built a gray, cedar shingled house here, which they named "Grarocks." Smoky blue shutters framed windows over the terrace at the rear of the house which overlooked a fabulous view of the Gulf of

Introduced from Japan in the late 1800s, the salt-spray rose, Rosa rugosa, delights visitors with its perfumed flower and bright red fruit.

Atlantic Shore Line to the Gun Mounts

The front of the Graves' cedar shingled home, 'Grarocks', was approached by a long driveway from Route 1A.

Maine. Guests were greeted at the front door facing inland, where masonry pillars flanked the drive. "Grarocks" had ten rooms altogether with a separate double garage containing a second floor apartment. The Graves' daughter, Robin, was married here at "Grarocks" in 1941. Sadly this home, like the Stevens', was razed in 1942. Beyond the next turn in the walk a gazebo was built to further enhance this magnificent summer home. It is interesting to note that these, like most other Odiorne Point properties, were owned by women. This was relatively unusual at the time and came about when shaky economic conditions threatened family property and wealth in the late

17

'Grarocks' had ten rooms and two bathrooms. The terrace at the rear of the house bordered on rocky shore.

Area of the Graves' house today. Nothing remains of the house 'Grarocks' today in this view of where it stood. The house was leveled during World War II with the U.S. Army occupation of the land.

Atlantic Shore Line to the Gun Mounts

Graves' gazebo. On the outermost point of land, Dr. Graves built this summer house.

1920s and '30s as many men had their assets acquired in or transferred to their wives' names in an attempt to forestall seizure.

The islands you see from this point are the Isles of Shoals. The farthest island to the right (with the lighthouse) is White Island. This island was the childhood home of the famous poet Celia Thaxter: it became a part of Odiorne Point State Park in June 1992. As you look left from White Island, the next island you see is Star Island. On most days you will be able to make out a large white building on Star Island, the Oceanic Hotel, built in the 1800s and currently used for summer retreats by the Unitarian-Universalist and United Church of Christ Churches.

The next large island to your left is Appledore, the largest of the archipelago. In the 1800s Appledore

A rare glimpse of pre-war social life at Odiorne Point. Robin Graves' wedding reception at 'Grarocks', the summer of 1941.

Atlantic Shore Line to the Gun Mounts

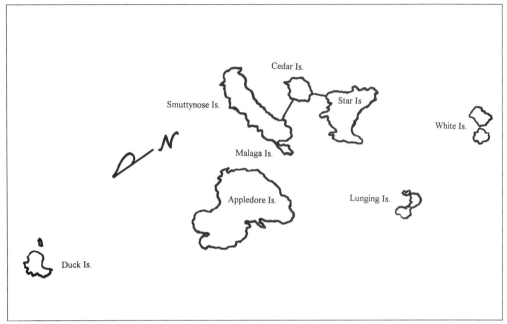

Sketch of the Isles of Shoals with perspective from the Panama mounts.

Island was the cultural center for summer visitors in New England. Celia Thaxter, by then a well-known poet, created a mecca for writers, artists and leaders of that era. Among others, she was hostess to fellow writers Walt Whitman, John G. Whittier and Nathaniel Hawthorne, to artist Childe Hassam and to New Hampshire native President Franklin Pierce. Appledore Island is now the location of the Shoals Marine Laboratory, an undergraduate marine science educational facility run jointly by Cornell University and the University of New Hampshire. A little to the left of Appledore, you may be able to see low-lying Duck Island. During World War II Duck Island was used by the military as a practice target. Today Duck is home to cormorants and gulls and is the southern-most breeding site for Harbor Seals.

21

Look further to your left along the horizon, and you might be able to see the faint gray lighthouse tower of Boon Island. This is the setting of Kenneth Roberts' 1956 historical novel "Boon Island" and the midwinter fight for survival of shipwrecked sailors.

At your extreme left, at the mouth of Portsmouth Harbor, is Whaleback Light. Built of granite in 1872, this light marks the harbor's entrance. Beyond Whaleback, in Maine, is Fort Foster, built for defense in 1896. It became part of the coastal system to defend the Portsmouth Naval Shipyard during World War II. Upriver you can see the bright white tower of Portsmouth Harbor Light in New Castle. This light is built on the foundation of the pre-revolutionary Fort William and Mary. Renamed Fort Constitution, the

Standing by the Graves' stone wall, a view towards the left finds the 59-foot Whaleback Lighthouse marking the entrance to Portsmouth Harbor.

Atlantic Shore Line to the Gun Mounts

fort defended the harbor during the Revolutionary and Civil Wars, World Wars I and II, and is currently the site of a Coast Guard Station.

You might also see large ships entering or leaving the harbor. Often these ships will stand just off this point waiting for the right tide and the arrival of a pilot to take the ship up the Piscataqua River. The Piscataqua has very rapid tidal currents and eddies which require highly skilled navigation.

The open water you see is not the Atlantic Ocean: it is the Gulf of Maine. One of the most biologically productive bodies of water in the world, the Gulf is bounded on land by the Canadian provinces of Nova Scotia and New Brunswick, and the states of Maine, New Hampshire and Massachusetts. Its ocean boundaries are Georges and Browns Banks, underwater "hills" which keep the water of the Gulf circulating in this "sea within a sea." The Gulf waters have only one major connection to the North Atlantic Ocean waters, the channel between Georges and Browns Banks which are about 200 miles to the east of the Isles of Shoals. Because so many rivers empty into the Gulf, the waters are less salty than those of the Atlantic and have a counterclockwise circulation pattern. The physical boundaries of the Gulf cause some of the highest tides in the world, varying from 7 to 10 feet along Cape Cod to as high as 50 feet in Canada's Bay of Fundy.

Odiorne Point's rocky shore provides some of the best tide pools from Massachusetts to Maine. Students and visitors flock here to unlock the mysteries of the tide pools.

As you continue along the rocky shore, you can see some fine examples of the geologic forces that formed this land.

As scientific methods improve and new information becomes available, our understanding of the earth's geological history is refined and rewritten. As late as the 1950s, it was thought that the continents had always been where they are: continents did not move. Today, geologists agree that continents are slowly, continuously moving. The northeastern United States, maritime Canada, and indeed the rocky shore in front of you, have played a major role in providing knowledge and an understanding of how the earth was formed.

Atlantic Shore Line to the Gun Mounts

Rocks are geologists' textbooks. Reading Odiorne's rocks you can see examples of the massive slabs of crustal rock (called plates) that churned up from the molten core of the earth and moved about its surface over hundreds of millions of years. In this process, known as plate tectonics, these plates repeatedly collide and tear away again, always changing shape and size. The northeastern United States is a jumbled result of at least three major collisions of these plates, which thrust up mountains that were at least as high as Mt. Everest or K-2 are today. The Appalachians, Taconics, Berkshires, Green Mountains and New Hampshire's White Mountains but have since been eroded over aeons to their present heights of between 4,000 and 6,000 feet.

In this small area, an experienced guide can unravel the geological wonders of Odiorne Point.

25

Seen from the Panama mounts, this cove contains the roots of ancient trees together called 'The Drowned Forest'. The tower in the background was a visual observation post used to aim the guns at Odiorne Point. To the left of the tower is a tall siren, part of the emergency warning system of Seabrook nuclear power station.

Geologists estimate that the last wrenching separation from North America occurred about 200 million years ago, tearing away parts of plate to form Greenland, Scotland, Scandinavia, and even Northwest Africa. After all this stretching, tearing, uplifting and glacial erosion, two types of rock are predominant: metamorphic schist and basalt (which was once volcanic magma). The presence of rock formations like those at Odiorne in Africa helps us track the movements of these giant plates throughout time. As you look out over this rocky shore, just imagine the power needed to break apart a giant plate of these rocks and move it thousands of miles away!

In addition to plate movement, glaciers were a potent force in determining the shape of the land upon which you walk today. Twenty thousand years ago,

Atlantic Shore Line to the Gun Mounts

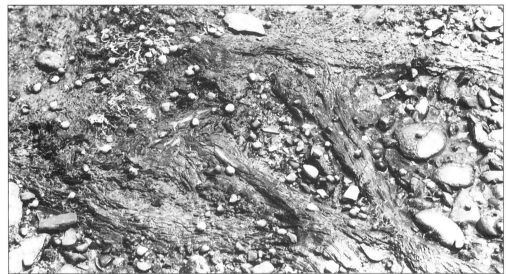

Roots of trees that lived some 3,500 years ago are exposed at low tide.

Odiorne Point was covered by a mile of ice, the weight of which pushed the land down some 1,300 feet. The glacier drew water from the ocean, lowering sea level by about 500 feet. This altered the shoreline so that about 13,000 years ago the shore was 20 miles west of Odiorne Point. If the coastline were there today, Route 125 near the Lee traffic circle would be ocean-front property. As the glacier retreated, the land rebounded, and terrestrial life returned. One fascinating piece of visual history here which helps us understand these changes is the "Drowned Forest". A forest of trees extended to the east from here to the Isles of Shoals and perhaps beyond. Using carbon dating, geologists have determined that 3,400 years ago the ice-age glaciers had melted enough that the sea had risen close to its present level, drowning the trees. Trunks and root systems of these trees may be seen today at low tide in the "Drowned Forest" at the southern rim of the park.

27

Footprints in Time

Gun Mounts to Battery 204

The history contained at Odiorne Point spans an almost unimaginable expanse of time. As the pathway bends to the west, you will jump ahead to another time: World War II.

On your right is a fairly well-preserved structure that appears very much like a large goldfish pond surrounding a sometime fountain. Actually it is a gun position, one of four in this part of Odiorne Point. With England under full assault and Germany on the verge of controlling all of the North Atlantic sea lanes, the

The wheels of the 155mm guns rested on the center raised portion of the Panama mount.

28

Gun Mounts to Battery 204

Although not taken here, this is a photograph of a 155mm gun. Four of these guns were mounted on the Panama mounts at Odiorne Point.

US War Department formulated plans for US coastal defense in 1940. Upon the United States' entry into the war in December of 1941, these plans were implemented immediately. Odiorne Point was critical in protecting the Portsmouth Naval Shipyard, and Fort Dearborn was established here to defend the harbor at its entrance. The first installations were 155-millimeter (approximately 6-inch diameter) guns which were rushed to Odiorne's shore and installed here. Although these guns lacked the power to fire a shell the desired distance (they were designed in World War I as field artillery pieces), they were the only ones available for immediate installation in critical coastal positions. In the spring of 1942, four such guns were placed on these "Panama" mounts which were named for the place of their origin. Two more of these mounts directly ahead of you have been filled in. The fourth is completely obscured by vegetation.

This early defense installation was augmented quickly with underwater listening devices, three rows of mines and a submarine net across the mouth of the harbor. Waterfront searchlights, barbed wire and machine-gun positions on the shore also contributed to the defense system. Two additional gun positions were constructed at Odiorne Point: Battery 204 near the Science Center and Battery Seaman on the north side of the park. (You will see these later in your walk.)

From the gun mounts look south along the coast: you will notice a high tower about a mile away. It is an observation control tower for sighting enemy vessels. This tower is one of a string of high points which stretched from Halibut Point (Cape Ann), Massachusetts to Kennebunk, Maine. Not all of these were continuously manned, but could be activated if

The end of the patrol area for the lifesaving station at Wallis Sands was located near the Panama mounts. Using a key located at this station, lifesavers would 'punch' the time clock to record the time of their visit. Look closely to the left of the center of the photograph - the 'U.S.S. Constitution' is just visible.

Lifesavers are shown meeting in this photograph from a glass plate negative. Note the snow on the men - it appears to have been placed here - perhaps to show how rigorous their duty was.

needed. As you look out to the Isles of Shoals, you will see another of these towers on Appledore Island (the largest island toward the left).

On the northern shore of this cove, a very small piece of ground was purchased in 1894 by the United States. On it a small check-in station was built marking the northern end of a foot patrol from a life-saving station at Wallis Sands Beach over a mile to the south. From 1894 into the 1930s, men walked this stretch of shoreline watching for "mariners in distress."

Take another turn on the asphalt path and as you head back toward the parking lot, you pass the site of the Eastman's house and barn.

Cyrus and Charles Eastman of Littleton, New Hampshire, built them here in the early 1870s and had a subdivision plan prepared in 1875. In that plan they proposed to sell small lots of land to potential summer cottage builders. However, they sold only one large plot, on which no building was ever constructed. The balance of the property remained undeveloped and was sold in 1906. The new owner, Charles F. Shillaber, realized no further sales of the subdivision and sold it fourteen years later.

In 1921, Robert Sugden purchased Shillaber's entire parcel. He had already bought the property immediately to the north and then had updated subdivision plans drawn for the "Shillaber" parcel. Sugden moved the old Eastman house and barn west to the edge of what is now Route 1A, remodeled the barn into a house and sold both. He also sold four lots to the Graves family, and his widow, Bertha Sugden, sold six

On land bought in 1874, Mr. Cyrus Eastman built this Victorian house.

Gun Mounts to Battery 204

lots to the Stevens, the sites of which you passed on your way to the gun mounts.

The Eastman house was purchased from Mrs. Sugden by Fannie Botsford in 1933 and opened to paying guests that summer as a tourist home called "Glen Gables." The renovated barn was bought from Bertha Sugden in 1927 by Florence Keller, who held it until 1939. She in turn sold it to Mary K. MacKinnon on behalf of George S. Howard, who established it as the 1620 Club, a reputed gambling establishment.

Walking along the asphalt path on the east side of the parking lot, you will notice you are approaching a high man-made mound overgrown by sumac and pine trees.

This mound did not exist before 1942: it is Battery 204, the second largest of Fort Dearborn's gun batteries. As you look about you, it is hard to believe that prior to World War II, there were flat open fields and continuous ocean views from almost any place on the peninsula.

The Eastman House was moved to what is now route 1A and became 'Glen Gables' when bought by Mrs. Fanny Botsford in 1933. This postcard is advertising accommodation for overnight guests. Note how open the area was then.

Battery 204 to the Dolphin Fountain

Battery 204 was just one of many such batteries of a continuous coastal defense system. These batteries were all built from common plans and were positioned along the Atlantic coast from Maine to the Caribbean and along the Pacific coast from Alaska to Panama. Two 6-inch, "rapid-fire guns," one mounted on either side of the casemate (commonly called a "bunker"), could fire 138-pound shells about 15 miles out to sea, over twice the distance to the Isles of Shoals. The

Under this mound of earth is World War II Battery 204. On the left side you can see one of its three ports.

Battery 204 to the Dolphin Fountain

One of the two 6-inch guns of Battery 204. Note the two 'humps' along the shore by the trees on the left side of the photograph. That area is enlarged in the next photograph.

observation post atop the bunker along with others from Cape Ann, Massachusetts, to Kennebunk, Maine, provided the "eyes" for the guns of Odiorne in the pre-radar years of the early 1940s.

The inside of the bunker was a honeycomb of rooms for shells, gun powder, and target plotting, plus a large electrical power room. Just recently it was learned that this battery may be unique. Unlike most other batteries, the coast artillery crew had direct, inside access from the bunker to the observation post.

The huge 16-inch shells that you see at this bunker are for the much larger gun position as we shall discover later.

Keeping the park toll booth to your left, proceed directly across the driveway. As you approach the woods on the far side of the field, a glance back will reveal the central port of Battery 204 through which

35

An enlargement of the previous picture shows the 155mm gun installation covered by camouflage netting and the ammunition magazines.

all materials were brought into the bunker.

In the meadow before you, as well as in many other open spaces throughout the park, an exquisite lacy flower may be found that has many interesting facts and legends associated with it. This abundant plant is

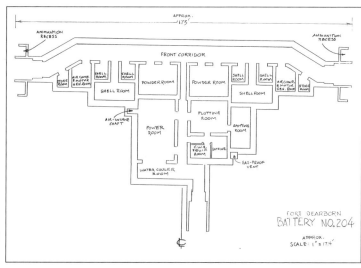

A sketch of the interior of Battery 204.

Queen Anne's lace, also called, and rightfully so, wild carrot. For centuries this species was eaten in Europe and early America, but was stringy and needed hours of cooking. During the early 1900s the value of vitamin A from these wild carrots was realized and scientists developed this stringy, bitter, tough plant into today's lush garden vegetable. As the legend goes, this plant was growing in Queen Anne's royal garden and being an accomplished lacemaker, she challenged her ladies-in-waiting to a contest of reproducing the flower in lace. Since it would only be proper for a queen to win her own contest, you can readily see why it is known as Queen Anne's lace.

The center entrance to Battery 204 today.

Dolphin Fountain to the Odiorne Homestead

Rounding the end of a low fence and curving to the right, you will follow a path through the field about 100 yards or so to a point where a second path diverges to the right. This path leads you to a masonry structure: the "Dolphin Fountain" of the Marvin/Straw estate.

Look closely at the center section and you will see a scallop shell and dolphin cast in relief. From the dolphin's mouth you see a metal pipe, which was the fountain portion of this structure. In the 1920s and 1930s,

The Dolphin Fountain as it existed prior to World War II. Water trickled from the mouth of the cement dolphin.

Dolphin Fountain to the Odiorne Homestead

a small windmill some distance to its rear brought well water to the fountain: the stones flanking the fountain were benches.

To its left stood a stucco summer home that is called the Marvin/Straw house for the last two families to summer here. This house, built around the turn of the century on a reputed "old cellar hole," had five owners in all. We have come to know it best through the memoirs, written and oral, of Marjorie Marvin Hartford, who spent idyllic summers here with her family from 1920-37 in the house she called "Sea Acres." Just to the right of the Dolphin Fountain is a remnant patch of ancient roses. These "Apothecary Roses" could have been the earliest cultivated roses brought to New Hampshire. Though still surviving, the tree shade discourages their fragrant deep pink bloom.

Marvin/Straw house. This house passed through five owners. We now know it best by accounts and photographs by Marjorie Marvin Hartford who lived in 'Sea Acres' from 1920 to 1937.

The Dolphin Fountain as it is today.

A 1937 real estate advertisement for the house described "Sea Acres" as a "desirable estate ... with spacious grounds attractively landscaped" and a long sun porch on the front, screened in summer and windowed the rest of the year. Its first floor had a large living room, dining room, butler's pantry, servants' dining room, kitchen, and laundry. Upstairs were five "master" bedrooms, a den, a bathroom, two servants' bedrooms, and their bathroom. Six large fireplaces graced the house, which had a separate garage, stable and "man's" room. The 1937 asking price was $17,000! The price had dropped during the Depression from $25,000 in 1920. It is interesting to note that the advertisement for the sale of the land also stated "The sanitary arrangements are excellent, there being a 500-foot sewer with a 7-foot drop leading beyond and emptying below the low water mark." The remains of that

Dolphin Fountain to the Odiorne Homestead

Standing by the fountain today, we are surrounded by trees. Prior to World War II mowed lawns and fields permitted sweeping views down to the sea.

This is the carriage house of the Marvin/Shaw house, which can be seen behind the trees to the right. The carriage house, which included 'man's quarters,' was later used as a garage.

pipe can be seen today along the shore. Before you leave the Marvin/Straw estate grounds, look at the dense growth of trees and brush behind the fountain. Most of that growth was not here in the 1920s and '30s and standing here during those decades, you would have had a clear view of the ocean.

Turning your back on the Dolphin Fountain, take the path that angles slightly to your right, and you will emerge onto the asphalt bicycle path. You will be following this path for several hundred yards. (Watch out for cyclists, and roller-blade skaters!)

Just as you reach the bicycle path, you will see twin masonry pillars at either end of the Marvin's Norway maple-lined, semi-circular driveway. Just as the Marvins did, volunteers plant geraniums and other

One of the two sets of masonry gateposts which marked the entrance to the Marvin/Straw house from Route 1A. Volunteers plant flowers atop these posts every spring.

Dolphin Fountain to the Odiorne Homestead

These Norway maple trees line what was once the semi-circular drive for the Marvin/Shaw house.

flowers in the pillar tops each summer. Turn to the right onto the bicycle path on a slight downward grade, and stop when you are opposite the driveway in front of a white house across Route 1A.

FOOTPRINTS IN TIME

The Odiorne Homestead to the Pond

The buildings here are those of the Odiorne Farm. The house, at least, dates from 1800. According to family history, this was the third house built by the Odiornes in an unbroken occupancy of 282 years, ending with the government's taking of the land in 1942 to build Fort Dearborn. In 1657, John Odiorne was a resident of Portsmouth. At that time Portsmouth included Great Island (New Castle) and much of Sandy Beach (Rye) as well as parts of other adjoining communities.

The 1800 Odiorne farmhouse as seen today from the bicycle path.

The Odiorne Homestead to the Pond

As a Portsmouth resident, John Odiorne could take part in a 1660 "division of public lands."

Whether the land he purchased then included all of today's park property or only some portion has not yet been determined. When his estate was divided after his death in 1707, no mention was made of land on the peninsula (he had previously deeded it to his son). However it did include 41 acres "in the Plains" (near the southern end of Islington Street in Portsmouth) and 3 acres "at Great Island." Creditors of John Odiorne received eighteen shillings and three pence for each pound (twenty shillings) due.

Born in Sheviock in Cornwall, England, Odiorne was said to be a fisherman on Smuttynose Island of the Isles of Shoals who "was granted" 42 acres on Great Island shortly before his purchase of land at Odiorne Point (according to the Odiorne genealogy). Hannah,

Ralph Edwin Odiorne, holding a pitch fork, at the Odiorne family farmhouse about 1903. Compare the front doors, aside porch and trees in the two pictures of the house.

the first born of John and Mary (Johnson) Odiorne, married a Lt. John Batson of Saco, Maine. In an attack in Maine in 1703, American Indians captured the then-pregnant Hannah and her two children and took them to Montreal! Batson died in captivity in 1704. Two years later James Stilson, who had heard of Hannah, went to see her and purchased her release. They were married in October 1705.

At first, the Odiornes made their livelihood by commercial fishing, farming, haying the salt marsh, and trading with the American Indians. They later developed a more comprehensive farm which prospered enough so that, by 1800, fifth-generation Ebenezer was able to build the house you see across the road. Complete with a large barn, carriage house, shed and well, the house faces south over what then were gently

Odiorne carriage house, left, and shed, right. The shed, in disrepair, still exists today.

The Odiorne Homestead to the Pond

Members of the Odiorne family and other early settlers are buried in this cemetery to the west of the Odiorne farmhouse.

sloping fields. The position of the house kept winter's northeast blast to the rear wall. To the west of the house on a small rise, the Odiorne fishermen dried their catch on crude wooden platforms called flakes, giving that area the name "Flake Hill."

As the farmstead developed, the Odiornes needed more tools and built a blacksmith shop. A small family cemetery, possibly the oldest in New Hampshire, is still on the property and allegedly also contains the remains of early settlers and some American Indians with whom the early Odiornes had dealt peacefully. Many graves can still be found in the cemetery, which was deeded to the Colonial Dames of America in the State of New Hampshire. A granite monument to the first settlers was dedicated in 1899 by their organization. Originally the monument had been placed near the shore, but it was moved to the cemetery in 1955

47

FOOTPRINTS IN TIME

A gravestone in the Odiorne family graveyard.

to enable continued viewing while protecting it from vandalism.

In later years, parts of the farm were leased to others for haying, fruit orchards, potatoes, and other ground crops. The family had moved elsewhere and returned only in the summertime after 1915.

At the close of World War II, the federal government offered to sell back the property west of Route 1A to Ralph E. Odiorne. In his seventies, and settled in Massachusetts, Mr. Odiorne was unable to take advantage of the offer. By a sealed bid, the property and the entire marsh to the west were purchased in 1949 by Ralph Brown. An ardent conservationist and amateur historian, Mr. Brown restored much of the house and barn that had been unkindly altered by the military during World War II.

Well to the southwest of the farmhouse is a concrete-block structure, a powder magazine from World War II. This, the use of the farmhouse as a barracks, plus an infiltration training course comprised the primary uses of the farm as part of Fort Dearborn.

In the 1990s, Mr. Brown gave the western half of the marsh to the [Town of] Rye Conservation Commission and sold the balance to the State of New Hampshire. All of it is to be kept in a natural state. As of this writing, Mr. Brown still occupies the house, and has life-tenancy, so please do not go onto the farm property without his permission.

While few Odiornes still live in the Seacoast area, descendants of John Odiorne now live throughout the United States and Canada. The names of early

Business card for the Odiorne Point Tavern about 1925.

Odiornes echo in its history as farmers and fishermen, in foreign and domestic commerce, as ship owners and masters, sailcloth manufacturers, leaders in the colonial assembly and in the state legislature in the early decades of our Republic.

Turn away from the homestead and look along the shoulder of the cycle path to your right. You will see a narrow pit-like depression. From its center grows a small stand of quaking aspen: it is, in fact, a man-made pit.

In 1838, the Odiorne Point land owners petitioned the selectmen of Rye to construct Columbus Road to the sea just north of here. This road provided access to the shore for small-boat fishing and for inland farmers to collect seaweed as fertilizer for their fields and gardens.

Columbus Road as it appeared in the 1920s.

The Odiorne Homestead to the Pond

What remains of Columbus road today. Near this high point of land some believe that David Thomson built his 'Great House'. Gravel from this hill was removed at the turn of the century to construct what is now Route 1A.

Take a few steps farther along the path and, still on your right, you will see the scarred face of a hill, the highest natural elevation on Odiorne Point. This marks the site of a gravel pit. The Columbus Road of 1838 went over this crest, but in 1902 the state had mounted a project to extend the shore road (now Route 1A) to the south, cutting into this hill for gravel. Of itself, this was hardly a momentous event, except that the gravel pit is, by oral tradition, the site of the first house in New Hampshire. Unfortunately any traces of this dwelling probably would have been obliterated by this excavation.

Around 75 yards along the cycle path you will see a pond behind the fence to your right. Like the road builders before them, the builders of Fort Dearborn dug their gravel pit here in the 1940s; gravel from this pond was used to construct Battery Seaman (you will

Cars on Route 1A in the 1920s.

come to that Battery soon). Fed by the springs of Odiorne, this pond provides a freshwater habitat for wildlife and is an interesting place for study. Before its excavation this pond was a gentle slope on the farm of Mrs. Janette Gage. Mrs. Gage's son, Edward, was the friend of Arnold Whittaker who dreamed of owning a chicken farm, but needed a place to establish it. Through his friendship with Edward, Arnold was permitted to use part of a huge barn and the sloping land as his chicken farm. When the federal government descended on Odiorne in 1942, he was given only thirty days to remove his chickens, in spite of a wartime ban on interfering with food production. However, move he did to a farm he found in Stratham, New Hampshire, taking thousands of chickens with him.

The Odiorne Homestead to the Pond

Despite his efforts, Arnold's dream came to an abrupt end in 1958. The chickens contracted a contagious disease, and he had to destroy the entire flock. Whittaker moved to an island in Yarmouth, Maine, where he acquired a captain's license and a reputation as a good navigator. In 1961, he was offered the contract for ferry service from Portsmouth to the Isles of Shoals' Star Island. Whittaker bought the M/V Viking in Long Island, New York, in order to carry out that contract. Today, Captain Bob Whittaker, Arnold's son, is the owner and principal captain of the Isles of Shoals Steamship Company.

One of the seven major habitats of the park, this fresh water pond was created during World War II by excavating the soil for other purposes. Springs keep water in the pond.

53

Pond to the Salt Marsh

Odiorne Point is fascinating for its natural history as well as offering a visual representation of the earliest New Hampshire history. In some ways it is possible to see the area even as the first settlers would have seen it by looking at different natural features. If you are taking this walk between late August and early October you will see splashes of yellow blossoms in every open field. Look closely; in addition to goldenrod, you will see an abundance of tansy. Notice its cluster of button-like yellow flowers: it is a strewing herb. A native of Europe, this herb was brought here by early settlers and is now a common weed in North America.

This path, which parallels Route 1A, is enjoyed by bikers and walkers most of the year and cross country skiers in the winter.

Pond to the Salt Marsh

Settlers scattered tansy inside on their earthen floors and outside along their foundations because it was a deterrent to lice, mosquitos, and other insects. Break off some leaves and crush them. Its pungent odor is another attribute: it is a deodorant! Since the early colonists washed their clothes infrequently, an odor fighter of any degree was no doubt welcome.

Tansy leaves may be steeped to make tansy tea, but since it is a sedative, too strong a brew can be dangerous. If you have an itchy mosquito bite, rub the crushed leaves on it, and you can experience the sedative value of this very useful plant. By rubbing your face and arms with the leaves, it will help repel mosquitos.

Salt Marsh to Heritage Garden

Continuing along the bicycle path look across the marsh to where, toward the right, Route 1A crosses Seavey Creek at the wooden bridge. Try to picture a working tidal mill there. The Pine Tree Mill had been operated by William Seavey and John Foye until they sold it to the Odiornes as a grist and saw mill in 1842. Operation continued until 1863, when the mill burned and was not restored. As you continue along the path, you will see expanses of open salt marsh to your left. This marsh played an important role in the settlement of the area, and continues to be an important marine

Salt water marsh seen from bicycle path. The western side of the park is almost completely bounded by saltmarsh. The Odiorne family operated a tidal mill near the bridge in the 1800s.

Salt Marsh to Heritage Garden

Salt marsh hay was stacked upon wooden posts called staddles to keep it dry at high tide and to allow its removal by boat or by wagon when the marsh was frozen.

habitat within the park and along the coast. The first settlers chose Odiorne Point for many good reasons. There was plenty of stone and wood for building and, in the surrounding marshes, rich marsh hay for their animals and for roof thatch. Just as important were the many fresh water springs of Odiorne Point. As the demand for hay increased, new approaches were required to move the harvested hay out to market. For this, gundalows were utilized and bog shoes for horses and oxen were designed.

At first, the gundalow was nothing more than a "dumb barge," no rudder, no sail, no deck, no deck house, all of which were added in later years. These water-going carriers were pressed into all sorts of service until roads were cut through the forests. Marsh hay was harvested and piled to dry on circles of pilings

Flat bottomed boats, called gundalows, were used in the Odiorne Point area to haul salt marsh hay and supplies.

called staddles, remains of which can still be seen in some marshes along the New England coast. Transferred to a gundalow and brought to the soggy shores of creeks, the hay was pitched onto wagons pulled by horses or oxen wearing bog shoes. They served as a kind of "snowshoe" and were fastened to the animals' hooves to spread their weight and prevent them from sinking into the marsh.

You can see strings of old fence posts along the edge of the marsh creeks. These cedar posts mark the "Dead Line" at the rear of World War II Fort Dearborn. Any intruder found inside that line was to be shot! A former soldier mused if the fencing here were not primarily devised to keep the military in rather than intruders out.

Salt Marsh to Heritage Garden

As you continue along the path, you will pass a gravel road with a (usually) closed gate to Route 1A. This is Frost Point Road. Residential estates once lined this road, and the estate owners used it to get to the northernmost point of Odiorne. For now, your walk passes this road: we'll rejoin it later.

During World War II, the salt marsh perimeter of Fort Dearborn was enclosed by these posts strung with barbed wire to prevent the entry of unauthorized personnel. This photograph was taken after Mr. Brown purchased the property; his name, R.L. Brown, appears on the post sign.

Heritage Garden to the Plotting Room

Continue north on the bicycle path just over 100 yards, past one narrow path on your right to a much broader, well-defined lane on your right. Flanked by stone walls, this was the private driveway to the Foye/Whitcomb House. As you begin the walk up the drive, a clearing on your right marks a flower garden.

The roses here were once famous: people would drive past the garden just to smell the resplendent blooms. Today, park volunteers have lovingly restored

In several areas of the park you will notice meadows such as this. They are created by controlled mowings to provide a habitat for plants and animals.

Heritage Garden to the Plotting Room

Foye/Whitcomb garden today. Volunteers have maintained Mrs. Whitcomb's garden. The rows of tall trees on three sides of the garden demonstrate what happens to a privet hedge if not clipped.

Steps in Whitcomb stone wall. These steps and the garden are the only evidence of the Whitcomb home that remain today.

FOOTPRINTS IN TIME

At the foot of Whitcomb steps are these huge rocks that were put into the wall to retain the terrace.

much of the garden, and named it the (Foye/Whitcomb) Heritage Garden.

The drive ends in some broken asphalt left from World War II. Directly ahead are some foundation stones hidden in the grass and brush which are fun to explore. At first just a small farm house; buildings, sheds, and barns were added by the Foye family over the decades. Paul and Kathleen Whitcomb purchased the property and named it "Pioneer Farm." When the government descended in 1942, "Pioneer Farm" was a twenty-four room estate and it served as an example of the undervalued payments received from the government by the eleven home owners of Odiorne. The elegant home and over 41 acres of land were purchased at the price of only $23,500!

Mr. Whitcomb and his mother (his father had died

62

earlier) owned a chain of restaurants, "The Baltimore Dairy and Lunch", with (allegedly) locations in New York, St. Louis, New Orleans, Minneapolis, and other metropolitan areas. At least some of the seats in these eateries were like the school chairs with one enlarged, desk-like arm. This feature, probably not unique to the Whitcomb diners, gave rise to the epithet "one arm lunch."

A wealthy man, Paul Whitcomb would arrive for the summer with two Locomobiles, a phaeton and a limousine: very expensive cars. In the later '20s and '30s his wife, Kathleen, (who suffered from epilepsy) and her brother, Luther Robie, both from a Nashua, New Hampshire building supply family, began to live here year-round with one "Denny" Driscoll as caretaker.

Foye farmhouse. Built about 1800 by the Foye family, several generations of the family farmed the land until the early 1920s.

Whitcomb Home. The Foye house was bought by the Whitcombs in the early 1920s and many modifications were made to the house and the barn.

Entrance to the Whitcomb's 'Pioneer Farm' in the 1930s. Mrs. Whitcomb's garden is seen to the right of the driveway.

Plotting Room to Battery Seaman

At this point you should turn toward your right and as the broken asphalt becomes a dirt path, another man-made hill looms up on your right. Although bunkers for smaller guns included a self-contained room for plotting targets, sensitive targeting instruments could be damaged by the earth-shaking concussions from the firing of the huge 16-inch guns. For these larger guns, a separate plotting room was needed several hundred feet away, and such a plotting room was built within this bunker. Telephone land lines from the 50-mile web of observation posts to the north and south converged here. Target coordinates were called in and the plotter would calculate the correct aiming points for the guns. The ports of this bunker are now barricaded with huge stones.

Due to their historic interest the New Hampshire Division of Parks would like to open all of the bunkers to the public, but the twin problems of vandalism and of funding to make them safe have thus far prevented such an undertaking.

The stone walls that you can see here were built with the rocks and stones unearthed as the then-open fields were developed and houses built.

FOOTPRINTS IN TIME

At a slight rise in the path as it circles to the northerly end of the plotting room, you will see on your left the junction of stone walls and a large area of trees. This is a miniature upland forest habitat, the fourth habitat type you have encountered on your walk. Deer and fox have been spotted here as well as in other wooded areas of the park. If you are quiet you might see one, especially in the fall when there are fewer park visitors to frighten them away from open areas and paths.

On your right, a path leads to the top of the plotting room bunker where air vents from the rooms below are still in place.

During your walk you may discover a unique plant growing in the meadows that looks like a rosette of very furry leaves. As the summer progresses, a tall stalk covered with small yellow flowers will develop and may grow several feet tall. Mullein was brought to North America from Europe and was well established by 1800. You may know this fuzzy plant as "quaker rouge." Because Quakers were not allowed to use makeup to enhance their complexion, they rubbed their cheeks with Mullein leaves. The little barbed hairs caused an irritation that reddened their skin and gave the desired effect of rouge without breaking any rules. Local Indians quickly discovered that lining their moccasins in the winter with this naturally occurring "fur" was a great way to insulate their feet against the cold.

Plotting Room to Battery Seaman

Continue along the well-trodden path around the bunker as it dips and begins a slight rise into a group of very rough-barked trees. At the largest of these shagbark hickories, around 100 yards along, the path you should follow makes an abrupt left turn. After another dip and rise, the nearly straight path will deliver you back to Frost Point Road about 100 yards east from the bicycle path.

Turn left on Frost Point Road. A small hill along the left side of the road was the cover over pumping equipment for an underground reservoir, which was built to provide fire-fighting water to hydrants located in and around Battery Seaman.

Just beyond the blocked-up command post entrance you pass through woods that contain many shagbark hickory trees.

FOOTPRINTS IN TIME

After 100 steps or so the southerly port of the two 16-inch gun positions will come into view on your right. You will return here, but for now proceed along the road. Note the heavy growth of bittersweet on the bunker. This plant, along with all the other fast growing shrubs and trees, was planted here by the U.S. Army Corps of Engineers to camouflage the bunker .

The raised banking on the left side of the road covers a series of end-to-end foundations which can be seen on a Corps of Engineers map. It is believed that this series of foundations accurately locates "the farm that grew." Property and a small house built by George Frost in 1759 was purchased by Stephen Foye in 1799: the cottage is shown on an 1805 map. John Seavey Odiorne bought the small farm in 1842, but his early death led to its sale to Captain Thomas R. Clark only eight years later in 1850. Capt. Clark enlarged the house to two stories, and opened a boarding house. Boarders were taken in, and sleighing parties were entertained in winter. However, neither Clark nor his successor, Captain George W. Towle, were able to make a financial success of the boarding house.

George Pierce purchased the property in 1868. He and his brother James, both of whom had experience on a Vanderbilt yacht and at the Rockingham Hotel in Portsmouth, further expanded the house by adding a "substantial" wing. They opened the "Sagamore House" as an elaborate country inn. Their enterprise flourished and a second wing of three stories was built

Plotting Room to Battery Seaman

Elegantly appointed Sagamore House attracted notables in the early 1870s.

for the 1870 season, during which Cornelius Vanderbilt was a guest. While they prepared for the 1871 summer, a fire broke out in the kitchen and, accompanied by much confusion with the Portsmouth Fire Department and a breakdown of its equipment, the hotel was gutted by the fire, except for a separate bowling alley.

Only partially insured and deeply in debt, the Pierces were unable to rebuild. James moved to San Francisco, while George remained on the property, living in all that was left of their once-prosperous inn, the bowling alley. Finally, in 1889, the property was sold to Dr. W. Duncan McKim of New York.

Battery Seaman to Frost Point

The large port to the bunker on your right is the central port for Battery Seaman. Into this port shells, gunpowder, and other supplies were moved; half to the right, half to the left. A little farther on the northerly gun position will come into view, but you will pass it by for now. Continue until you emerge into an open area with a panorama of Little Harbor on your left. From here you can see the town of New Castle, Fort Stark and the Wentworth Hotel straight ahead, Whaleback Light on your right, and Kittery Point, Maine on the

Taking the path to the top of Battery Seaman gives spectacular views on a clear day. Here are Little Harbor and the Wentworth Hotel.

Battery Seaman to Frost Point

Fort Stark and Whaleback Lighthouse. The white building to the left was the World War II Harbor Entrance Control Post. To the right is Whaleback Lighthouse.

other side of Portsmouth Harbor behind Whaleback Light.

This is Frost Point, named for the family who owned and squabbled over it during the last half of the eighteenth century. The farm, including some marsh, was acquired during the mid-1700s by George Frost. Leaving others to farm his property, Frost moved in 1770 to Durham, New Hampshire, where his children were raised. The first judge of Strafford County, he suffered a stroke in 1794. A few months later, he deeded the entire farm at Odiorne to his younger son, John. When the judge died in 1796, an older son, George Jr., his sisters and their husbands joined in a suit to have the deed voided. The trial ended with John still in possession of the property.

George initiated a second suit contending that the

stroke had left his father with unsound judgment. In the end, the court directed John to sell the land to satisfy the interests of the others. In deeds of March, 1799, John sold segments of the land to John Foye, Stephen Foye and Ebenezer Odiorne. Although John lost all of his property, the land kept his family's name: Frost Point.

Walk down the path on your right to a point, marked by a breakwater completed in 1903 by the US Army Corps of Engineers. Together with a second barrier from the shore of New Castle's Fort Stark (on the opposite side of the harbor), this breakwater protects the entrance to Little Harbor. Today dozens of pleasure boats find sheltered moorings here in the summer. The breakwaters have created the sandy shore stretching

Frost Point breakwater. Completed in 1903, this breakwater protects Little Harbor. If you walk along it, note the shallow sandy bottom on the harbor side and the deeper rocky bottom water on the seaward side.

Frost Point sandy beach. Probably formed and protected by the Little Harbor breakwaters, this sandy beach adds to the varied habitats of the park. Many family picnics were held here before the war.

several hundred yards to the left on this side of Little Harbor. The sandy shore is the fifth different habitat you have encountered in your walk.

Sheltered only by the natural "breakwaters" of the land in 1623, this haven is the accepted anchorage of the ship "Jonathan" early in that year. The arrival of this ship marks the beginning of the first European settlement in what is now New Hampshire by thirty-one-year-old David Thomson. Thomson led the small band who arrived on the "Jonathan" to establish a settlement and trade with the local Indians. The fishing vessel "Jonathan" made several voyages to the settlement as did the "Providence," bringing additional settlers, provisions and news from England.

David Thomson's story is told in two versions, the first of which is a narrative blending the works of

The earliest known map of the Piscataqua River, c.1660. European explorers found friendly American Indians in this area. (Courtesy British Museum Library)

chroniclers of early New Hampshire. In these accounts, Thomson worked as a young clerk in the Plymouth (England) offices of the Council for New England. Two council members, John Mason and Ferdinando Gorges, gained a joint grant to the area from King James I. They conferred a patent on Thomson for 6,000 acres presumably including today's Odiorne Point, New Castle, and perhaps the area which would become Strawbery Banke and later Portsmouth. For his part, Thomson was to fulfill for Mason and Gorges terms of their grant from the King: that they "... shall and will before the expiration of three years ... have in or upon the said portions of lands or some part thereof, one part with a competent guard and ten families of his Majesty's subjects resident and being in and upon the said premises ...."

Exactly where Thomson's settlement and trading

Battery Seaman to Frost Point

post was located probably will never be known. As you recall, one site suggestion is near the pit-like depression across from the Odiorne homestead you passed earlier in your walk. It is, by oral history, the site of the first European house in New Hampshire although there is no proof that is the site. Unfortunately, that place was disturbed when the gravel pits were dug for road and World War II fort construction. It is now unlikely that even a proper archaeological dig would produce any evidence to confirm the location of New Hampshire's first house.

The second account of Thomson's settlement was published by two descendants of Thomson in 1979. This newer account contends that Thomson came here more than once before 1623, first in 1607 as an apprentice to a seagoing apothecary, Dr. Richard Vines, and later as a representative of the Council of New England to build a fortified position as a foothold for England in "Northern Virginia".

Also by this account, Thomson's building, Pannaway Fort, served as a haven for fishermen of the Isles of Shoals in the "off season." (Pannaway is an American Indian word meaning "place where the waters [of the ocean] spread out" into the marshes.) Samuel Maverick wrote in 1666 of his alleged visit in 1623, that the fort was "... a strong and large house, enclosed with a large and high palizado and mounted gunns ..." Some have argued that this fort was actually at New Castle, not Odiorne. That argument is weakened by accounts of guns later being hurried from England to protect a fishing community at Fort Poynt (New Castle). The guns were needed to protect the community following a raid by the pirate Dixie Bull in 1632. Further, if Pannaway Fort were built before 1623, it is reasonable to believe that it was built on the ocean-facing shore of Odiorne rather than inland. A coastal position would enable them to bombard Spanish or French ships that might attack the "Northern Virginia" settlements of England.

Further, through several decades of the settlements around the Piscataqua basin, Pannaway acquired the name "Rendezvous Point." This epithet referred not to the land here, but to the practice of mariners along the northern coasts to form into convoys; the better to protect themselves from pirates, privateers and the Spanish and French. It is possible, of course, that both accounts of the first settlement bear elements of truth: that the first construction was of a "fort," and that, when Thomson brought his family to Pannaway, he built a separate home, or a "great house" for them. This home may also have served as a trading post for commerce with local Indians with whom he was known to have been friendly. Although we do not know exactly where it was, we do know from their accounts that the settlement was begun and was visited by a number of contemporaries. Miles Standish came to Pannaway Fort in its first year. He sought much-needed supplies to sustain New Plymoth until the next English ship

Battery Seaman to Frost Point

arrived there with additional provisions. David Thomson returned with Standish to Plymoth, only a day's sail in good weather.

Perhaps it was on this trip or in the course of earlier exploration of the coast with the apothecary, Dr. Vines, that Thomson spotted an island in Massachusetts Bay. In 1624, he was charged by his English "masters" with helping Samuel Maverick build at present day Chelsea "... a small fort ... placing four murtherers (cannon) to protect him from the Indians ..." This task reintroduced Thomson to Massachusetts Bay and its "planters."

England was once more preparing for war with Spain, and support by the Council of New England for Pannaway sagged. Thomson's interest was renewed for the island he had seen in Massachusetts Bay, and he began building a trading post there in 1625. The following summer he moved his family and a few servants there, leaving his 6,000-acre patent behind.

In 1627 and early 1628, the "old planters" around Massachusetts Bay were alarmed by the antics of one Thomas Morton. Trading guns and liquor with the Indians for furs, Morton turned Mt. Wollaston into the unbridled rowdyism of Merry Mount. "... drinking and dancing about many days together, inviting the Indian women for their consorts ..." according to New Plymoth's Governor Bradford. Scandalized, the "old planters" prevailed upon Bradford to suppress Morton. The cost of the action to seize and deport Morton was

FOOTPRINTS IN TIME

shared by the settlers, and Mrs. Thomson was listed as a contributor in the amount of fifteen shillings from Thomson's Island, a name the Boston Harbor isle retains today.

The time and place of David Thomson's death are unknown, but Amias' name on the list to deport Morton presumes that she was a widow at the time of Morton's extradition. New Hampshire's first settler had led an active and adventurous life in the short span of only thirty-six years. Thomson's widow subsequently married Samuel Maverick and kept house for him, their three children, and his mother. They moved to Noddle's Island (East Boston) in 1633 and remained there until 1650. Subsequently, the Mavericks lived in Saco, Maine, and in New York City, where Maverick finally was able to escape the "life-long tension between his Church of England loyalty" and "the grim and forbidding mien of the separatist Puritans."

Frost Point to Battery Seaman

Now you should turn away from Frost Point, and retrace your steps to the flat ground on the road. As the dirt path begins to change to a gravel road, take the less frequently used trail to the left in front of the bunker. This path takes you along the shore-side of Battery Seaman to the northerly position of the two 16-inch guns which were contained in this battery.

With the success of the Allies in Europe by 1944, a July moratorium was declared on coastal-defense construction. Test firing of the guns of Battery Seaman

Photograph of a 16-inch gun taken at the Aberdeen Proving ground.

(Battery 103) was scheduled on June 19, just short of this moratorium. Bad weather postponed the test until June 21 because the concussion of the huge guns would be amplified by "heavy" weather. A contingent of the 22nd Coast Artillery Regiment was sent to the Wentworth Hotel in New Castle to open windows and remove art and statuary from vulnerable spots! Perhaps you saw the hotel on the other side of Little Harbor, a large white building with two faded red-roofed towers. Three shells were fired from each gun and the sound and vibration were "plainly felt in Portsmouth and Kittery." According to one unsubstantiated report, tradesmen spent many days replacing window glass at the Wentworth in spite of precautions to protect them.

Walk past this northerly gun position to its twin in the south. A small path on the right of the bunker

One of the Battery Seaman guns firing in 1943. Note the camouflage paint and lack of vegetation.

Frost Point to Battery Seaman

Fresh water marsh from on top of Battery Seaman

leads up onto the top of this casemate, and the magnificient view from the "summit" make the detour very rewarding! The view from the top is one of the best of land and sea, from the salt marshes that feed into Little Harbor, Portsmouth Harbor, up the Maine coast and out to the Isles of Shoals. You will also have a full view of the enclosed fresh water marsh which is in front of you on the ocean side. This is an unusual habitat to be so close to salt water. During the spring and fall it is alive with migrating birds, providing a source of fresh water for shore birds and a home for fresh water marsh plants and animals throughout the year.

Proceed into the gun port. The circular rails you see in the ground mark the gun's actual position. The thick roof and overhang above you were designed to withstand a considerable bomb or shell strike. The

81

One of the two guns at Battery Seaman.

ceiling still has some rusting cleats from which a monorail hung to bring the 2,240-pound shells from storage to the guns. As you continue on through the port, stop at the metal door on your right and peer through the openings. The subdued light you see filtering through is from the northerly gun position 500 feet away.

Battery Seaman to the McKim/Gage Property

When you emerge from the battery you will return to Frost Point Road. Turn left and retrace your earlier steps about 100 yards. There a triangular patch of grass on the left marks the entrance of the driveway to a house built around the end of the nineteenth century by Dr. W. Duncan McKim. He was the one, you will remember, who bought all the land from the Pierces

Fresh water marsh. In severe northeast storms this fresh water marsh, located to the southeast of Battery Seaman, will turn brackish due to salt water intrusion.

Dr. W. Duncan McKim built this sixteen room house in 1892 which he called "Sagamore Farm."

In 1894 Dr. McKim built this barn behind his house.

after the "Sagamore House" burned down. This was a large house with two matching sides separated by a porte cochere (a carriage drive-through) which went through the house to the large barn behind. The barn itself had two ells, one of which was large enough to house Dr. McKim's 40-foot pleasure boat in winter. Down at Little Harbor he built a 100-foot pier and a house nearby. With an organ valued at several thousand dollars, his wife, Rogé, an accomplished musician, gave organ recitals in this lovely "Organ House."

Proceed up this driveway, noting the parallel rows of sugar maples which line the drive. Farther up, look carefully and you will see gateway posts of stone. If you take a detour to the right you will find the house and outbuilding foundations, but it will take a thorough

A closer view of Dr. McKim's barn.

search to find these ruins. The McKim house and property were sold in 1918 to Mrs. Janette W. M. Gage.

It was Mrs. Gage, who in 1924, had the large piece of acquired property subdivided for sale. She sold all the lots along the shore of Little Harbor from Frost Point to the Whitcomb property.

In addition to the McKim/Gage house, other summer homes stood on two of the subdivision lots. At the harbor end of Frost Point, a handsome two-story masonry and wood house was built by retired Chief Justice (New Hampshire Supreme Court) Robert J. Peaslee. A lot with Mrs. McKim's "Organ House" was purchased (excluding the organ) and expanded somewhat by Mrs. Helen M. Waldron. The Peaslee house survived during the war as (according to one unconfirmed report) the residence of the commanding officer of the 22nd Coast Artillery Regiment. Dilapidated, it

In the late 1800s, Dr. McKim built this cottage to house an organ for his wife. An accomplished musician, she gave many recitals here.

Battery Seaman to the McKim/Gage Property

These maple sugar trees were planted by Dr. McKim along his driveway.

This huge stone near the sugar maples shows the polishing action of the glacier that covered the area during the last ice age.

was razed after the war as a safety precaution. The Waldron cottage had stood near Battery Seaman and it had to be razed after the war since the concussions of the test firings had ruined the "Organ House".

The story of how Odiorne Point became a state park is an extremely interesting one. The large Gage house had been one of eleven homes taken by the government at the outset of World War II. At that time, both the written laws and verbal representations of federal agents promised the landowners the opportunity to reacquire their properties when the government no longer needed them. The Government continued to use the land until 1959, when all the acreage east of Route 1A was declared surplus.

However, in 1949, a federal law had been enacted outlining new rules for disposition of federally acquired property. Once the Department of Defense had no fur-

The Waldrons converted the organ house into a cottage with a new wing, running water, and electricity. The family's cat appears to be welcoming the photographer.

Battery Seaman to the McKim/Gage Property

In 1933, retired Chief Justice of the New Hampshire Supreme Court, Judge Peaslee, built this stone and wood house at Frost Point.

ther need for such properties, other federal departments were offered the land. If the land was of no use to the federal government, it was then made available to state governments and municipalities, in that order. Only after all public agencies declined the properties was it offered at auction to the public, including but not limited to the original, private owners. Although a number of bills were passed in Washington D.C. to override this law for the properties in various other areas around the country, one to favor the Odiorne Point landowners passed the Senate but failed to be reported out of committee in the House of Representatives.

The landowners of Odiorne waged the Battle for Odiorne under the strong leadership of Edward Gage (by then a lawyer). Despite valiant efforts to get their homes back, they failed in their challenge of more

Edward A. Gage II and his dog, Ski, in a 1918 Model T Ford depot wagon in 1935. Edward Gage later played an important role in trying to get the government to sell Odiorne land back to its pre-war owners.

powerful interests. Their properties were sold to the State of New Hampshire in 1961 for $91,000 with the proviso that the land be used as a park. After a decade of inactivity the state was prodded by a group of private citizens to do something about the natural and historic promise of Odiorne Point. Led by conservation activist Annette B. Cottrell, a series of studies was prepared and, in 1972, Odiorne Point was dedicated as a state park. The park was going to be named Fort Dearborn State Park. However, just before it opened the name was changed to Odiorne Point State Park to recognize that family's long association with the land.

The years of World War II began badly for the twenty-four families who owned property at Odiorne Point. There had been rumors, of course, but no one who

Battery Seaman to the McKim/Gage Property

knew the quiet elegance of living here could quite believe that this land would be needed to defend the Portsmouth Naval Shipyard. After all, there were Fort Constitution, Fort Stark and Fort Foster: that should be enough.

Unfortunately, the shipyard was far more important to defense planners than Odiorne families realized. Especially hard hit were those eleven families who owned homes at Odiorne; even more so the few who lived here year around. Within a few weeks after the December 7th attack on Pearl Harbor in 1941, the landowners of Odiorne Point knew the worst. They received notice that they had to vacate their properties and remove all their goods: they were given only a month to do so! Some furnishings of absentee owners were removed to an old warehouse in Portsmouth, where subsequent ravages of leaking roofs and vandalism reduced them to ruin. It cannot be said that any property was surrendered happily! Many owners, in fact, were so shocked by the low valuation placed on their estates that the government was forced to go to court to have their properties condemned. This slowed the transfer process so much that some properties were not legally owned by the government for over a year after the families had been ousted.

Having commandeered the land, the Army Corps of Engineers and private contractors immediately set about converting Odiorne Point into the primary defensive position guarding the approaches to the

FOOTPRINTS IN TIME

A sketch of the World War II Portsmouth Harbor defenses. Fort Dearborn was a key element in those defenses.

shipyard. Route 1A was closed from Brackett Road on the west nearly to Wallis Sands on the south. The "Dead Line" barbed wire fencing was strung in the marsh and along the shore (you saw fence posts in the marsh), and machine guns were placed at critical points. Building of the fortification began at a frantic pace.

As the fort went up, houses went down: among the first to go were several summer homes. Meanwhile, construction proceeded with deliberate speed on additional gun positions. Together with the 155-millimeter guns placed near the Drowned Forest, two 6-inch guns and two 16-inch guns were to be placed on the peninsula. In May 1943, the Odiorne Point area had a new name: Fort Henry Dearborn, in honor of a distinguished Revolutionary War general from nearby Hampton. One of the stories of the construction period highlights an ironic conflict between civil defense directives and the military's need to meet fort construction schedules. During the war, coastal and strategically important towns were instructed to "black out" by covering windows, painting the top half of car headlights black and a number of other ways to prevent any light from showing the enemy where land and targets were at night. The Portsmouth area was no exception. Army troops patrolled the waterfront of Portsmouth and civilian defense wardens saw to it that

92

Battery Seaman to the McKim/Gage Property

even the narrowest shaft of light was put out. Meanwhile Fort Dearborn was ablaze with lights for round-the-clock construction!

Fort Dearborn construction was completed in three years. Ironically, the guns of Odiorne were never fired at the enemy, and were obsolete as defensive weapons by the time of their completion in June of 1944. Perhaps only one of the 16-inch coast artillery guns (originally designed as naval guns) survived post-war scrapping. If you are ever near the Aberdeen Proving Grounds in Maryland, you can find a lone survivor there.

Park visitors often question the necessity for building these fortifications. Was the threat of coastal attack in the early days of World War II great enough to justify the large expenditure of money and manpower? Although the Germans had no aircraft capable of crossing the Atlantic to bomb the Portsmouth Naval Shipyard in early 1942, they did possess surface ships that were capable of shelling the coast from well offshore. Because most of the U.S. fleet was in the Pacific, these coastal guns became an important means of defense. Even in mid-1943 the Germans still possessed two major naval warships that could cross the Atlantic and shell the coast. By the end of that year, however, the threat no longer existed, but by then Fort Dearborn's fortifications were well on the way to completion.

Fort Dearborn certainly would have been a powerful

93

FOOTPRINTS IN TIME

deterrent to enemy naval forces had it been needed, and the Portsmouth Naval Shipyard proved well worth protecting. The shipyard constructed eighty-five submarines between 1939 and 1945. With a maximum employment in 1943 of over 22,000, the shipyard succeeded in launching three submarines in a single day, January 27, 1944!

With the end of the hostilities in 1945, the colors of the 22nd Coast Artillery Regiment were struck, and Battery Seaman (16-inch guns) and Battery 204 (6-inch guns) were dismantled, and the mines and submarine net were removed from the port entrance. Observation posts from Cape Ann to Kennebunk were abandoned, like hundreds of similar installations on the Atlantic and Pacific coasts.

Before 1900 this was the end of the road from Portsmouth. Horsedrawn carriages brought people here to enjoy the seashore. This was the site of the "Parking Lot" for the carriages.

94

The McKim/Gage Property to Columbus Road

As you proceed beyond the avenue of sugar maples the path winds over a ridge and eventually emerges from the woods to a magnificent view of the mouth of the fast flowing Piscataqua River. This overlook was the ocean-side end of Columbus Road, the 1838 road which you passed earlier in your walk, across from the Odiorne farm. It is now protected from erosion by the huge rocks placed here by the Army Corps of Engineers.

Taken in the early 1900s this photograph is of the monument erected by the Colonial Dames at the end of Columbus Road. It was later moved to the Odiorne family cemetery. The large white buildings on the left are the Wentworth Hotel.

Seaward end of Columbus Road. The road from Portsmouth turned towards the ocean on Columbus Road.

There are many fresh water springs on the Odiorne peninsula, but none in a more unusual spot than the one among the rocks near the high-tide line, below and a few yards to the right of this overlook. Early fishermen from the Isles of Shoals probably had to come to the coast to replenish their water supply. If they found this spring, it certainly would have been more convenient to get to than those inland.

This beach is fascinating to explore. As you walk farther along the path, look for the remains of the sewer pipe from the Marvin/Straw house. Another quarter mile along the edge of the rocky shore returns you to the rear of Battery 204, and, on your left, the Seacoast Science Center.

In 1973, the Audubon Society of New Hampshire sent a naturalist to conduct nature programs in a build-

The McKim/Gage Property to Columbus Road

ing the military had used as a fire station. This was the first public/private partnership at Odiorne. Audubon, a private, non-profit organization worked with New Hampshire Parks and Recreation in opening a summer nature center. When that building was removed, the Sugden House, which had been used, it is said, as a war-time officers' quarters and later as a park manager's residence, became the Park's visitor center in 1976. This center was managed by a third sponsor, the University of New Hampshire Cooperative Extension/Sea Grant Program. In 1985, a fourth sponsor, The Friends of Odiorne Point State Park, Inc., joined the other three to help oversee the programs at the Visitors' Center and in the Park. The Friends

Amongst these rocks runs a fresh water spring that is submerged at high tide.

Annette Cottrell Teaching Steps. Teaching steps constructed in honor of Mrs. Annette Cottrell recognize her many contributions to the establishment of the Odiorne Point land as a state park. It incorporated the landscape of Battery 204 in its design.

spearheaded a fund-raising effort which raised $1.2 million dollars to build the Seacoast Science Center. It opened its doors June 13, 1992. Retaining the Sugden House as its primary exhibit was a prerequisite of all designs for the Center. As the last private residence on Odiorne Point, it has a prominent place in the story of the park.

In 1920, Robert I. Sugden, a prominent Portsmouth businessman, purchased nine acres from Mary J. Foye. There he built a handsome masonry summer home, employing local artisans. A rarity for those days, the house had electric lighting and appliances, although an early electric refrigerator apparently failed and had to be replaced with a traditional icebox.

The home had nine rooms on the first floor, including a large living room across the front facing the

The McKim/Gage Property to Columbus Road

ocean flanked by three sitting-room porches. From a central hall were three bedrooms on the north side, while a dining room, kitchen, and bathroom lined the south side. A recessed stairway could be lowered to lead to an additional pair of bedrooms and a sitting room on the second floor. The upper level, plus a two-car garage and some interior walls on the ground level were removed when the Science Center was built. When you go inside the Center's meeting room, look at the stone fireplace: you will see the Sugden's initial, S, in the masonry above the mantle. The fireplace still works and today is used during special programs and events.

Outside, wide lawns and flower beds surrounded the house. Because of the rocky shore, Sugden built a salt-

Mr. Robert Sugden's summer home built in 1920. Note the power pole behind the house.

water swimming pool. The pool was right at the water's edge and was filled by the incoming tide: the water retained by a shut-off valve as the tide ebbed. Enclosed porches running along the east, north, and south sides gave the Sugdens a grand view of the harbor approaches, lighthouses, islands and boating activity. There was excitement during prohibition when rum runners tried to land illegal liquor in the cove north of the Sugden House. A United States Coast Guard chase forced the smugglers to dump their cargo at sea, some of which later washed up south of Odiorne Point.

As a finale of this historical walking tour of Odiorne, you are invited to share the Sugden's sea view from the porches of the Sugden House, along with the history exhibits to be found there. Also, don't forget to

Mrs. Phyllis Sugden Frink, with her daughters Barbara and Madeline, sitting on the edge of the family pool.

The McKim/Gage Property to Columbus Road

Phyllis Sugden Frink, a progressive woman of the 1920s, at the wheel of the family's touring car.

Madeline and Barbara Frink, ages eight and five, outside their grandfather Sugden's house where they spent their summers.

Annette Cottrell Teaching Steps inscription. Mrs. Cottrell used these words to argue that the land we now know as Odiorne Point State Park should be preserved. Note the remnants of one of the 6-inch gun mounts by the picnic table.

visit the habitat exhibits in the Brown Exhibit Hall, to get a closer view of the many habitats you saw along your walk. We hope that this guide has helped you appreciate the many facets of Odiorne Point's cultural, natural and military history.

Bibliography

Brewster, Charles W., *Rambles About Portsmouth*, First Series, Portsmouth, N.H., 1859, Second edition 1873. Second Series, Portsmouth, N.H., 1860.

Brighton, Raymond A., *They Came To Fish*, Portsmouth, N.H., 1973

Clark, Charles E., *The Eastern Fronteer*, New York, N.Y., 1970.

Deane, Charles, *The Indenture of David Thomson*, paper written 1876. Text reprinted 1895 in New Hampshire State Papers, vol. 25, pp. 713-739.

Gurney, C.S., *Portsmouth, Historic and Picturesque*, Portsmouth, N.H., 1902.

Jenness, John Scribner, *Notes on the First Planting of New Hampshire*, Portsmouth, N.H.,1878. Reprinted 1895 in New Hampshire State Papers, vol. 25, pp. 663-673.

Levett, Christopher, *A Voyage Into New England and the Severall Townes Therein*, believed written in 1660. Text reprinted in N.E. Historical and Genealogical Register, vol. 39, 1885.

Odiorne, David W., Editor, *Genealogy of the Odiorne Family*, Revised Edition, Ann Arbor, Mich., 1967.

Parsons, Langdon B., *History of the Town of Rye, N.H.*, Concord, N.H. 1905. Reprinted 1962 and 1970.

Raymo, Chet and Maureen E., *Written in Stone*, Chester, CT, 1988.

Saltonstall, William G., *Ports of Piscataqua*, Harvard Univ. Press, 1941. Reissued by Russell and Russell, New York, N.Y., 1968.

Tallman, Louise H., *Odiorne Point: Highlights of History*, One of a series of educational pamphlets, Concord, N.H., 1973. Revised 1992.

Thompson, Ralph E. and Matthew R., *The First Yankee*. Privately printed, Salem, Ore., 1979.

Varrell, William M., Jr., *Rye on the Rocks*, Boston, Mass., 1962.

Whittaker, Robert H., *Land of Lost Content*, Dover, N.H., 1993.

Winslow, Ola Elizabeth, *Portsmouth, Life of a Town*, New York, N.Y., 1966.

Historical New Hampshire, New Hampshire Historical Society, Apr. 1948.

Articles:

King James and His Council of New England.

The First Planting of New Hampshire, J.S. Jenness (excerpts).

Notes Relating to David Thomson, Charles Deane (excerpts).

New Hampshire State Papers:

Vol. 1 - Early years, miscellaneous papers.

Vol. 17 - Transcripts of early documents.
Vol. 25 - Complete text of papers by Deane and Jenness.
Rockingham County Records, Court Records, Series A, Frost vrs. Frost; 1797 and 1799.
Register of Deeds, various deeds and plans.

Other Sources

Hassel-Shearer, Christi, *Odiorne Point Oral History.*
Project of Rye. Co-sponsored by Rye Historical Society, Rye Library, and the Friends of Odiorne Point, 1988.

Interviews on audio tape with:

Elizabeth *Howe,* Edward A *Gage,* Marjorie *Marvin* Hartford, Barbara Frink Hauck (*Sugden*), Paul *Hobbs,* Robin *Graves* Howe, Barbara *Odiorne* MacGregor & Priscilla *Odiorne* Newcomb, Ann *Waldron* Almendinger, Arnold *Whittaker.*

Ralph L. Brown, Nancy Odiorne Condon, Barbara Frink Hauck, Lt. Col. Wilbar Hoxie, U.S.A. Ret., Nelson Lawry, Arnold Silverstone, Annette Cottrell.

Friends of Odiorne Point State Park; History Committee: Howard S. Crosby, Chair, Nancy O. Condon, Bonnie Goodwin, Barbara F. Hauck, Richard T. MacIntyre, Stephen C. Miller, Lester Stevens, Louise Tallman, Phyllis Wilcox.

Photography:

Charles West
Howard Crosby
Thomas Arter
Wendy Lull

Nature drawings:

Sylvia Jones

Trail map:

Patrica Miller